I Am...

Precious Affirmations

Chantel Riley

Tellwell Talent
www.tellwell.ca

ISBN
978-0-2288-5960-4 (Hardcover)
978-0-2288-5959-8 (Paperback)

Dedicated to my nephews.
You both inspire me every day. May you grow
affirming yourselves as the Kings you are.
Auntie loves you.

I AM

PRECIOUS AFFIRMATIONS

written BY
CHANTEL RILEY

illustrated BY
JANICE BARBER

I am

LOVED

I am

COURAGEOUS

I am
SMART

I am
PEACEFUL

I am
CREATIVE

I am

CONFIDENT

I am

KIND

I am
ME

About the Author

Chantel Riley is a Canadian-Jamaican singer, songwriter, and actress known for her lead role as Trudy Clarke in the Canadian hit series Frankie Drake Mysteries. She also starred as Angela Cooke alongside Suits veteran Gina Torres in the Suits spin-off series Pearson.

Chantel kicked off her acting career after attending an open call in Toronto and landed her first gig playing Nala in Disney's The Lion King in Hamburg, Germany. After a successful one-year run, Chantel was immediately offered an opportunity to play this role on Broadway. In the summer of 2012, she made her debut in New York City and spent four years bringing this well-loved character to life.

Chantel officially launched her kids boutique called Sweet Riley! You can take a peek @lovesweetriley on Instagram. Getting her hands into the Kids Fashion industry has inspired Chantel to enter the world of literature and share her message of positive affirmations to young children all over the world.

CPSIA information can be obtained
at www.ICGtesting.com
Printed in the USA
BVHW021955190821
614611BV00044B/1139